THE WEATHER REPORT

HURRICANE WARNING!

EDITED BY JOANNE RANDOLPH

SUNDAY

MONDAY

TUESDAY

WEDNESDAY

THURSDAY

FRIDAY

SATURDAY

This edition published in 2018 by:
Enslow Publishing, LLC.
101 W. 23rd Street, Suite 240
New York, NY 10011

Library of Congress Cataloging-in-Publication Data

Names: Randolph, Joanne, editor.
Title: Hurricane warning! / edited by Joanne Randolph.
Description: New York, NY : Enslow Publishing, 2018. | Series: The weather
report | Audience: Grades 3 to 5. | Includes bibliographical references and index.
Identifiers: LCCN 2017001870 | ISBN 9780766090156 (library bound book) | ISBN 9780766090132 (pbk. book) |
 ISBN 9780766090149 (6 pack)
Subjects: LCSH: Hurricanes—Forecasting—Juvenile literature. | Hurricanes—Juvenile literature.
Classification: LCC QC944.2 .H84 2018 | DDC 551.55/2—dc23
LC record available at https://lccn.loc.gov/2017001870

Printed in the United States of America

To Our Readers: We have done our best to make sure all website addresses in this book were active and appropriate when we went to press. However, the author and the publisher have no control over and assume no liability for the material available on those websites or on any websites they may link to. Any comments or suggestions can be sent by email to customerservice@enslow.com.

Photos Credits: Cover, p. 1 muratart/Shutterstock.com (hurricane), solarseven/Shutterstock.com (weather symbols); series logo, NPeter/Shutterstock.com; interior pages background image, back cover, Sabphoto/Shutterstock.com; pp. 3, 28, 30, 32 Igor Zh./Shutterstock.com; pp. 4, 9, 14, 21 Neo Edmund/Shutterstock.com; pp. 5, 11 National Oceanic and Atmospheric Administration/Getty Images; p. 7 Science Source; p. 10 Joe Raedle/Getty Images; p. 12 XM Collection/Alamy Stock Photo; p. 15 Frederic Stevens/Getty Images; p. 17 Z2A1/Alamy Stock Photo; p. 18 Harvepino/Shutterstock.com; p. 20 © AP Images; p. 22 Spencer Platt/Getty Images; p. 23 Sandy Huffaker/Getty Images; p. 24 Biloxi Sun Herald/Tribune News Service/Getty Images; pp. 26–27 Michele Sandberg/Corbis/Getty News.

Article Credits: Carolynne Hutter, "In the Eye of the National Hurricane Center," *AppleSeeds*; Jan Adkins, "Hurricane Flight," *Ask*.

CONTENTS

CHAPTER ONE

A WHEEL OF WIND

Scientists don't know why hurricanes start, but they do know they form only over warm ocean water. Hurricanes start as **tropical** thunderstorms. The warm ocean water and the warm air above feeds the tropical storm through a process called **convection**. As the warm, moist air at the ocean surface rises, it cools. This cooling turns the water **vapor** in the air into drops of liquid water that form storm clouds.

More air moves in to take the place of the rising warm air, creating wind. The wind begins to spin counterclockwise, blowing the clouds into a spiral. Why does the wind spin? Because the earth rotates, giving everything on its surface a slight twist.

Hour by hour, for days or weeks, this wheel of wind spins faster and faster as it moves across the warm ocean, sucking in air from thousands of miles away.

The counterclockwise winds suck large amounts of moist air toward the center of the storm. This creates an "eye wall." The eye wall is where the air is then rapidly forced up into the **atmosphere**.

Because the atmosphere gets colder higher up, the air condenses from water vapor into cloud droplets. Those droplets either become rain droplets or go straight to ice crystals through a process called **sublimation**.

This satellite image shows a tropical storm forming in the Gulf of Mexico. Do you see the spiral shape of the clouds?

5

This whole process gives off energy that speeds up the winds and further develops the storm. The storm grows bigger as it gets caught in the spinning air. Dark clouds are pulled into the storm, causing the storm to whirl faster. Because the clouds are so high and thick, along with carrying tons of water, they block the sun and look dark for those of us on the ground. When the winds reach a speed of 74 miles (119 kilometers) an hour, the storm is called a hurricane. Fortunately, once a hurricane reaches land and is no longer over warm ocean water, it begins to lose its power.

THE STRENGTH OF A HURRICANE

Hurricanes can last for up to a week and range in width from 100 miles (161 km) to 300 miles (483 km). What is strange about hurricanes is that the center of them, called "the eye," is calm. As the eye passes overhead, it can fool people into thinking the hurricane is over.

Scientists use a scale of one to five to describe the strength of a hurricane. Category 1 is the weakest hurricane, with winds between 74 and 95 miles (119 and 153 kilometers) per hour (mph/kmh). This type of hurricane causes some damage to small buildings and trees. At the other end of the scale is a Category 5 hurricane. The wind speed is over 155 mph (249 kmh). This type of hurricane can destroy cities and towns.

Saffir/Simpson Hurricane Scale

Category	Definition
ONE	Winds 74-95 mph
TWO	Winds 96-110 mph
THREE	Winds 111-130 mph
FOUR	Winds 131-155 mph
FIVE	Winds greater than 155 mph

This chart shows the wind speeds of the different hurricane categories on the Saffir-Simpson scale.

THE EYE OF A HURRICANE

The ferocious winds of a hurricane spiral around the calm central eye. The fastest-spinning winds are found in the eye wall, right at the edge of the eye. You can make your own hurricane eye and eye wall. Fill a bathtub or large sink with 3 or 4 inches (8 to 10 centimeters) of water.

When you pull the plug, you'll see the water spiral around the drain. The water will spiral faster and faster as it goes down the drain, and when it is shallow enough, you'll be able to look right through the "eye" of the spiral into the drain. If you put your finger into the middle of this eye, you might not even get wet. The eye stays calm and the fastest-spinning water surrounds it, just like the eye and eye wall of a hurricane.

IN THE EYE OF THE NATIONAL HURRICANE CENTER

Because hurricanes can cause devastating damage when they hit land, scientists called **meteorologists** try to find them early and track them. The journey of a hurricane can begin far away. Along the coast of Africa, heavy thunderstorms concentrate into tropical clusters. Across the ocean in Miami, Florida, meteorologists at the National Hurricane Center use satellites to watch these storms develop and organize. These storm clusters, often called easterly waves, could be the beginning of a hurricane that will strike the United States.

A meteorologist tracks a hurricane at the National Hurricane Center. Experts try to figure out the strength and path of storms near the US coast.

The National Hurricane Center puts together prediction information on these deadly storms to help protect lives and property. It tracks weather in the Atlantic Ocean, Caribbean Sea, and Eastern Pacific Ocean. It provides advisories and alerts—called tropical storm and hurricane watches—for the United States and the Caribbean countries.

UH OH. . .

Meteorologists might track a disturbance that has moved across the ocean and into the Caribbean. Let's say it has grown into a tropical storm that is headed to the coast of Florida. Once the storm reaches tropical storm status (winds of 40 mph [64 kmh] or more), the National Hurricane Center names the storm, something like "Tropical Storm Ted." Names for tropical storms and hurricanes are names commonly used in North and South America. They alternate between male and female names.

This cluster of clouds is all that is left of Tropical Storm Erika, which broke apart over Haiti. It no longer has the spiral shape.

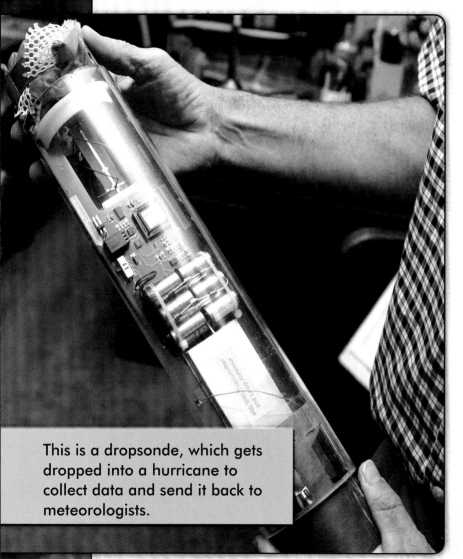

This is a dropsonde, which gets dropped into a hurricane to collect data and send it back to meteorologists.

12

HURRICANE HUNTERS

To get a closer look at Ted, the center sends airplanes into the storm. The pilots and scientists on board are called "Hurricane Hunters." They can determine the location, strength, and movement of the storm. They report their findings by satellite to the National Hurricane Center. The planes carry **dropsondes**, which are cylindrical tubes with parachutes attached that carry instruments and radio equipment. A dropsonde measures **air pressure, temperature, humidity**, and wind speed.

The National Hurricane Center also gets information about the storm from weather stations, ships, and buoys. When storms are about 100 miles (161 km) off shore, coastal weather radars provide important data.

The information and data from all these sources are fed into a computer to create models. These models predict the path and the strength of storms.

CHAPTER THREE

WHAT'S IT LIKE?

So what is it really like to be a hurricane hunter? Let's take a closer look. In Biloxi, Mississippi, a WC-130 Hercules rolls down the runway. The plane is so heavy with extra fuel for a long flight that it must build up speed for almost a mile (1½ km) before taking off. It carries a crew of six: two pilots, a navigator, a flight engineer, and two weather specialists. They are "hurricane hunters" from the 53rd Weather **Reconnaissance** Squadron of the Air Force Reserve, and they are looking for a hurricane.

Studying hurricanes by flying into one is a little like investigating lions by asking a lion politely, "Would you please eat me?" But weather scientists have been making these scary trips since the 1940s. Today, the information these scientific teams gather can be fed into powerful computers to help predict when a hurricane is forming and where it is headed.

The WC-130 Hercules is a large plane used by the US Air Force for weather reconnaissance.

5309

403 WG

Weather Reconnaissance S...

15

INTO THE STORM

What's it like flying into a hurricane? The outside edges of a hurricane are long arms of clouds curving toward the center. Inside the hurricane there are "cells," systems of rising and falling air. The big "Herk" flies into and out of dense cumulonimbus thunderclouds as rain streams on its "greenhouse"—the row of windows around the pilots. The ride is bumpy. Entering a cell, the plane will be swept down with the air, perhaps 1,000 feet (305 meters). A few minutes later, on the other side of the cell, rising air shoots the Herk upward just as fast. The pilots fight to keep the big plane on course.

The ride is worst when the plane gets close to the hurricane's center. The light is so dim and the rain so dense that the flight engineer can only see the engines closest to the cockpit. The ride now is not merely bumpy. It's like riding a bull in the rodeo. Everyone is strapped in tight. The noise of the engines and the hurricane is tremendous. The plane shoots up violently as it reaches the hurricane's inner wall.

Suddenly the big Herk bursts into sunny, calm air. It's now in the eye of the hurricane, a cylinder of clear air that is usually 10 to 20 miles (16 to 32 km) across. Above them, the hurricane hunters can see the

The back of the Herk is filled with weather instruments and equipment. The man in the photo is holding a dropsonde.

blue sky. Below them, water churns and swells. Around them, rushing clouds whirl, creating a "stadium effect" as the surrounding clouds rise up in a curving wall like the stands of a huge stadium. The pilot heads directly for the center of the eye.

The eye of the hurricane is clearly visible in this satellite image of Hurricane Patricia, a Category 5 hurricane that hit Mexico in 2015.

Both pilots watch the sea surface. "Now!" one pilot shouts into his microphone; they are directly over the center. The dropsonde is shot out of a launch tube in the belly of the airplane. All the way down and for hours as it bobs on the water's surface, the little disposable transmitter will radio air temperature, sea temperature, air pressure, wind speed, and wind direction back to the Herk and to the National Hurricane Center in Miami.

The crew and the Herk will punch through the hurricane three or four times in different directions during their eleven-hour flight, gathering information and plotting the storm's track before they fly back to their base. Soon, another big Herk will be on the way to ask the hurricane more questions, as scientists all over the world search for answers to the big, deadly mysteries of hurricanes.

DANGER ALERTS!

So, now back to our example storm, Ted. Hurricane hunters have been tracking its progress and whether it is getting stronger. The winds of Tropical Storm Ted are whipping around faster, and the National Hurricane Center has issued storm watches. It recommends that several coastal forecast offices be prepared to issue local warnings. Radio stations, television, and the internet all broadcast these warnings. The National Weather Service also broadcasts the warnings on its own NOAA radio, as well as on Facebook and Twitter.

The winds are now 75 mph (121 kmh), and Ted is officially a hurricane. Once a storm is within thirty-six to forty-eight hours of

The director of the National Hurricane Center talks to a news station about 2016's Hurricane Matthew.

landfall, the National Hurricane Center goes into high gear to communicate its forecasts and warnings to the public.

Because Hurricane Ted is heading toward land, towns along the coast are asking the people who live there to **evacuate**. Before they go, the people board up their houses to protect them from wind and flying objects.

DEADLY STORMS

Hurricanes aren't simple storms—wind and rain that roll over the hill and shake the trees for an hour or two. They are nature's skyscrapers, megastorms 8 miles (13 km) high and up to 500 miles (805 km) across. Hurricanes are weather extravaganzas that plug into the forces of the earth and spin like gigantic tops. They slide across the ocean, growing bigger, stronger, broader . . . until they meet the land and drain their great energy in destruction.

Meteorologists love hurricanes because they are wonders of nature. But if you're on a ship at sea or in a house on the beach, a hurricane is not

The winds and rain from Hurricane Sandy caused fires, floods, and power outages along the East Coast in 2012.

so pretty. The screaming winds and enormous waves can overturn a ship. At the shore, they can punch out windows, knock down trees, or pluck the roofs from houses.

The most dangerous part of a hurricane's destruction is flooding. Hurricane winds can push the ocean water toward shore, building it

The streets of New Orleans are flooded after a hurricane sweeps over the area.

up into a huge, rushing tide called a **storm surge**. Water level at the shore can rise 20 feet (6 m) in just a few hours. The deadliest hurricane in United States history happened in 1900, when Galveston, Texas, was struck. In the big storm surge more than six thousand people were killed. These days, with more and more people living in coastal cities,

Officials in Mississippi study the projected path for Tropical Storm Isaac as they make emergency plans for their community's safety.

experts predict that if a hurricane hit without warning, the death toll could be even higher. In low-lying New Orleans, for example, storm surge floods could completely cover three-story houses and wash away roadways.

But scientists have learned a lot about hurricanes since 1900. Meteorologists can now track the path a hurricane takes and predict where it is likely to hit days in advance. When Hurricane Isabel swept toward the North Carolina coast in 2003, the National Hurricane Center was able to make forecasts five days ahead, and scientists were off by only one hour in their prediction of where and when Isabel's eye would make landfall. The information collected by the hurricane hunters improves the accuracy of such forecasts by 30 percent—saving thousands of lives.

Off-Season

Hurricane season is from June 1 to November 30. It's an intense, exciting job for the meteorologists at the National Hurricane Center during this period. Tropical storms and hurricanes have to be watched twenty-four hours a day, so the meteorologists are always working.

NATIONAL HURRICANE CEN

NATIONAL WEATHER SERVIC

AT FLORIDA INTERNATIONAL UNIVERSIT

NOAA

DATES WIND PRESSURE DEATHS
UTC MPH MB
MAY 26-JUN 125 952
31

This board at the National Hurricane Center can get pretty busy during some months of the year, as meteorologists keep their eyes on storms around the world.

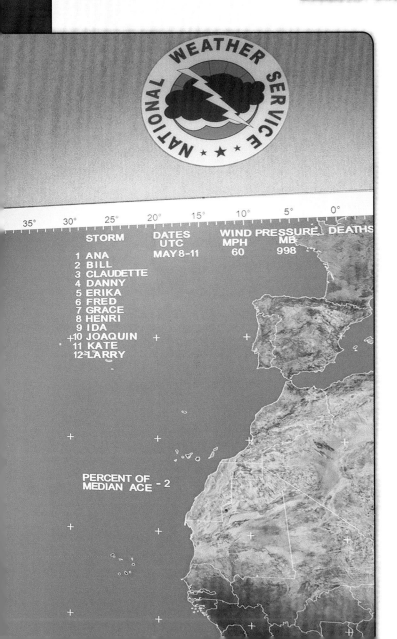

All year-round, scientists at the National Hurricane Center research and track hurricanes. They study data from all types of sources. The goal of these scientists is to understand hurricanes better, so they can improve their forecasts. Better forecasts can help save lives and properties.

GLOSSARY

air pressure The pressure placed on Earth by the weight of the air.

atmosphere The blanket of air surrounding a planet.

convection The movement of air or liquid caused by heat transfer. The hot air is less dense so it rises, while cooler air sinks.

dropsonde A disposable weather tool that has instruments for measuring different aspects of the weather. It typically has a small parachute to help it reach the ground safely once it is dropped from a plane.

evacuate To take a person away from a place of danger and bring to a safe place.

humidity The amount of water vapor in the atmosphere.

meteorologist A person who studies weather.

reconnaissance An inspection or exploration of an area to gain information.

storm surge The rising of the sea in response to changes in atmospheric pressure and wind during a storm.

sublimation The process of turning directly from a gas to a solid or a solid to a gas.

temperature How hot or cold something is.

tropical Relating to warm places.

vapor The gaseous state of something, such as water.

FURTHER READING

Books

Baker, John R. *The World's Worst Hurricanes*. Mankato, MN: Capstone Press, 2016.

Challoner, Jack. *Hurricane and Tornado*. London, UK: DK Eyewitness Books, 2014.

Lusted, Marcia Amidon, and Elizabeth Elkins. *Investigating Hurricanes*. Mankato, MN: Capstone Press, 2016.

Spilsbury, Louise, and Richard Spilsbury. *Top 10 Worst Hurricanes*. New York, NY: PowerKids Press, 2017.

WEBSITES

Hurricane Hunters Association

www.hurricanehunters.com/faq.htm

Learn more about the 53rd Weather Reconnaissance Squadron through
FAQs, pictures, and information on meteorology.

National Geographic: Hurricanes 101

video.nationalgeographic.com/video/101-videos/hurricanes-101

Watch a video from National Geographic explaining how hurricanes form
and how meteorologists track them.

Weather WizKids: Hurricanes

www.weatherwizkids.com/weather-hurricane.htm

Read more about hurricanes on this easy-to-follow site, which includes
charts, diagrams, and vocabulary definitions.

INDEX